For Gael

When you see me at the beach you may want to stare,

but my exclamation point is not from fighting off a bear.

There were wires, pumps, tubes, and I needed lots of care,

and everyone around me named me in their prayer.

The exclamation point is my symbol,
it's my battle scar.

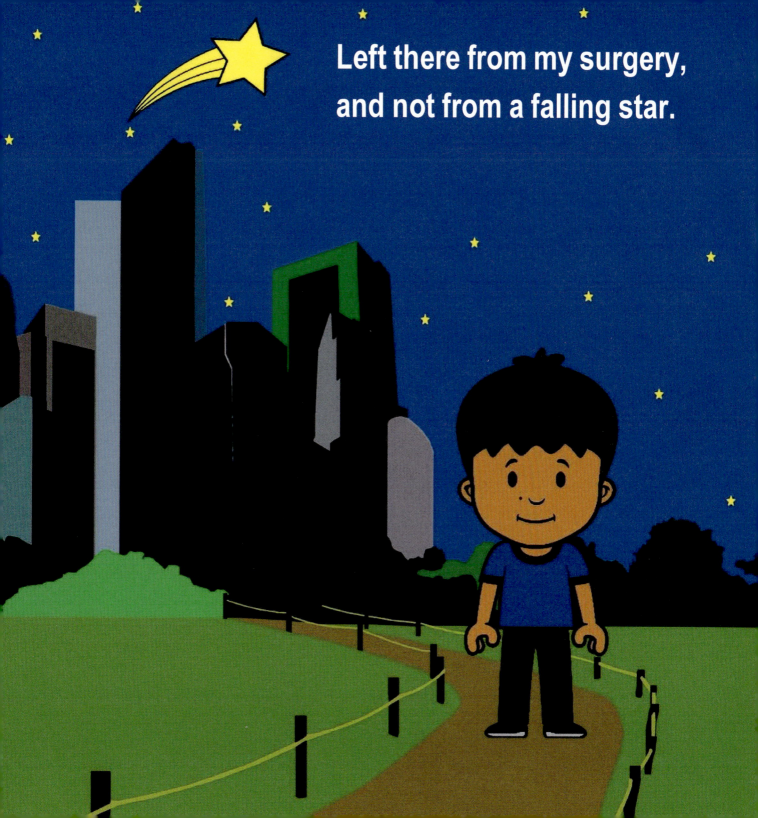

You won't know it just by looking, underneath my shirt it hides,

but trust me when I tell you on my chest it does reside.

It is pumping very well
behind my exclamation point.

I can hop, dance and play,
and I can even run!

About the time the doctors worked so hard to help my heart excel.

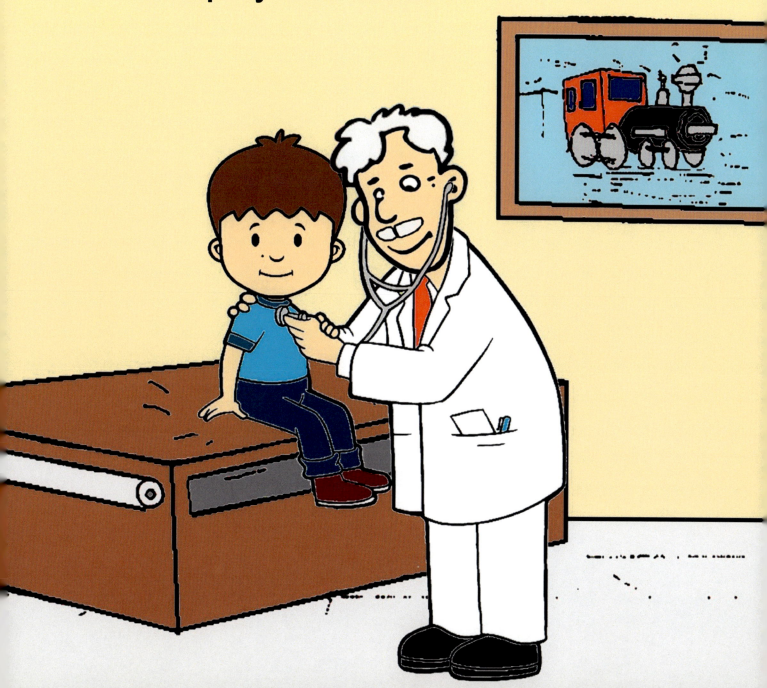

**So, let's go jump, skip, and spin,
and not give it another thought,**

Made in the USA
Lexington, KY
01 December 2017